THE HOME WITHIN US

THE HOME WITHIN US

ROMANTIC HOUSES, EVOCATIVE ROOMS

Bobby McAlpine

WITH SUSAN SULLY

MCALPINE TANKERSLEY ARCHITECTURE
McALPINE BOOTH & FERRIER INTERIORS

RIZZOLI
NEW YORK

New York · Paris · London · Milan

A hunting party sometimes has a greater chance of flushing love
and God out into the open than a warrior all alone.

—HAFIZ
(TRANSLATED BY DANIEL LADINSKY)

This work of finding the house within—and building it—is not something that is done alone or in a too serious atmosphere. It is a joyful collaboration of comrades in arms—architects, artists, artisans, other colleagues, and, most especially, our clients. Dreaming together, drawing together, building together, we connect what lies within our hearts to what surrounds it. Channeling the same thing, we form a family of sorts. Striking out on journeys—faithfully, carefully, ecstatically—we arrive at unforeseen destinations, and know them immediately to be correct. To those who travel this road with me, I give my heartfelt thanks.

CONTENTS

THE HOUSE WITHIN US

We are not all born to a compatible reality. I grew up in a series of Alabama sawmill towns comprised of pine bungalows and mill shacks built from the trees that had been felled to make space for them. Imagine a place where people don't actually own their houses—where there is little sense of proprietorship or care. Something always seemed missing. Because my father was a mill manager, there was an automatic schism between me and anyone around me, which made for a fairly lonesome setting. These were the things that turned me inward to weave a different world. I suppose you could say I dreamed my way out of the other one.

Since I was a little boy, I have been building the house inside me—and I'm still working on it. Because my childhood world was incompatible with my interior one, I created a paradise within. Traveling inside to fantasize and imagine things that were not there, I started drawing floor plans when I was five. One of my first was drawn in blue ink on the back of a Whitman's Sampler box. When I showed it to my mother, she said, "That's very nice, but the dining room is too far away from the kitchen." To this day, I still tend to make you walk across the house. Drawing floor plans in blue ink on hotel scratch pads, I still begin with what is on the inside of the house. Combing the interior tirelessly for math and order—and refining its responsiveness to the souls who will live there—I leave the outside for last.

What we crave in this life is an outer beauty that reflects the gorgeous world inside us. I am speaking about the house within us. What if the house inside you became the house you lived in? What if you envisioned that your life could be just the way you imagine it? Then you are en route to enlightened destiny, because each of us has huge control over our lives. We don't always realize this because we are, to a degree, defined by so many outside forces. But at the same time, we do have the power to create our own environment—and our environment, in turn, shapes us.

One of the strongest ingredients in keeping you *who* you are, your physical environment also keeps you in full awareness of *where* you are. If you can find your way to live in the house within you, then you not only create an enormous, broad, and lovely offering to yourself, but also to your "pack"—your family and friends. You will also inspire anyone who has not yet been able to make this connection. Such is the power of rooms.

THE CURATIVE HOUSE

Many artistic people come from backgrounds that are not artistic. Out of an innate desire to supply what is missing, we become writers or artists or architects. By morphing ourselves and our surroundings, we seek a cure for a condition we may not even consciously recognize. The world outside us issues an invitation to question reality, and ultimately it forces us home. Where is the place that mirrors our hearts? Where are we when we feel held and protected and whispered to? Where does the content of our intimate exchanges ring most true? By answering the questions of our hearts, the stronger among us become agents of change, making choices that advance the marriage of our interior and exterior lives.

I constantly bob in and out of two realities in an effort to make one look like the other. There is a lopsided chapel inside of me that I pace and study, and a closet full of props that I haul up to create a proper reality. It has a bottomless inventory and receives deliveries daily. Reaching down into it, I pull up trunks and baskets full of tapestries and candlesticks. Through heartfelt assemblage, these tools become markers that keep us from wandering too far away from ourselves, so my two realities do not become estranged.

I think of the house as *cure*, always—a safe place to mend from the demands of an insisting world.

One of my great joys is meeting the people I am going to work with—listening to them and discerning what they need. A certain spirituality, emotion, and mood is always present, like an undercurrent. I have built a computer in me that can hear this and understand what they require, even if it is for a need they may not know they have. By the end of the meeting, I know what house will be both diagnosis and cure.

When I'm talking with clients about this process, I explain that we really don't need to worry about what the house will look like. It will find its flesh once it finds its DNA. Formulating that very particular germ is imperative—only then can we shop the world to flesh it out. The heart and soul, ego and morality of the house within must be first discerned—the rest comes later. Once you have found that guiding spirit, it is an interesting and surprising journey to discover how the house will reveal itself on the outside.

BEAUTIFUL MATH

Home is a powerful means for healing. Designed correctly, the home is a very still and quiet place. When the math is gorgeous and perfect, it is at rest—and your potential to come to rest will follow. In so many of the places you normally find yourself, it feels as if you've put on a cheap suit with your pants twisted one way and your jacket the other, and you are trying to walk a straight line. But when things are right, and you are in an architecture that is strong and receiving of you, you are home safe and free.

Not as simple as symmetry and decoration, good architecture requires whole vision, expert timing, and sensitive placement. Rhythm and repetition, the question and answer of sequence, the clear-eyed invitation of good alignment—these are balm to any animal. The integrity of beautiful math is an elixir of spirit and place. Through gorgeous math good architecture creates a benevolent presence that pets and comforts you, or energizes and exhilarates.

Such houses have unique and personal disciplines that elevate you, holding you up to your own possibility. As much mirror as prescription, they are commissioned with the powers to soothe and to inspire. Like a good parent, their agenda is to draw your life forward with embraces and kisses and moments of great expansion that deliver you safely into the world. Always responsive and receptive, good math is another way a house says, "I love you."

WHY WE BUILD

Home is inside us—the place where we find everything that is true. We live now in the physical world, but our task is to walk in awareness of this inner place—to make manifest, in this world, evidence of another. In the land of brick and mortar we should always strive and struggle toward the likeness of our deepest understandings. We should seek that place that helps us to remember, or at least not to forget so quickly, the fleeting glimpses of truth that comes to us from within. The vulnerable beauty of this world fades to reveal its invulnerable source. I choose life, knowing it will perish. I choose love, knowing it may not last. This is why I love stone and steel and wood and thatch. Together, they are a marriage of the permanent and the perishable. There is a tender realism in their choice.

For many of us, the quest for home carries us through exhaustive search and compromise. Those who are highly attuned rarely succeed in bending the soul of a house they did not build to their will. A heart that is developed craves evidence of itself and the subtleties it has discovered. I dreamed of walking in the beauty and reality of my own mind. I had no place I recognized. This, in a nutshell, is why we build. When we finally find sanctuary in a physical edifice that mirrors our soul, it is ground gained and won—a flag on the moon of the heart.

I

HARMONY
OF OPPOSITES

To create spaces with a broad emotional spectrum, there has to be a pendulum that strikes far to the left and far to the right. A rhythm of the grand and the humble, the exhilarating and the calm, the bold and the tender must be struck at a regular rate. This can show up in a million different ways—in the scale of a room, the material, or the math.

People forget that animals love small spaces where they feel held and protected. Perhaps that is why I've always been drawn to humble, weathered properties, like little English inns or French country houses, where the ceilings are just above my head. A house seems to enfold you when the first room you encounter is such a space. Then, when you leave this protective pitch to enter an expansive room beyond, you encounter the opposite—an exhilarating sense of release.

This is why I often create alcoves to accompany big salons, which are beautiful but not always cozy spaces. An alcove or banquette provides an antidote to the loftier room. It extends an invitation that says, "Sit down inside of me and converse about something important. When you are ready to dance and expand and play, the space beyond is waiting."

Unexpected juxtapositions of materials also speak to the emotions. I love to combine stone and steel and wood and thatch. Because thatch usually sits atop something utterly durable—like stone or heavy timber—it appears ephemeral by contrast. It is a marriage of the permanent with the perishable, the invulnerable with the vulnerable. The pendulum, swinging as hard as it can to the left and to the right, cracks my heart wide open.

HOME

For the eyes are the scouts of the heart and the eyes
go reconnoitering for what it would please the heart to possess.

—GUIRAUT DE BORNEILH

(FROM JOSEPH CAMPBELL, *MYTHS TO LIVE BY*)

At the age of thirty-six, after several years of practice and many more of life, I realized that I had no place my heart recognized as home. Waiting for the exact invitation from the world, I had not found the perfect match. So I excavated from an active place inside myself—and I built it. I love the idea of taking your heart out for a walk and bringing it home.

In one of the few times I've drawn from a particular building, my house was inspired by Homewood, which Sir Edwin Lutyens built for his mother-in-law. With a lilting silhouette and a sideways entrance, Homewood is my favorite of all the houses he designed. I love the way the beautiful, bell-like roof huddles around the welcoming windows of its centerpiece to create a portrait. With broad shoulders and a simple face, it embodies both the humble and the statuesque.

Inside the house, I experimented with a style I call "monastery modern." By removing certain elements, I discovered that I could create a shell that is both elegant and spiritually quiet. There are no crown moldings, no window casings—not to keep the interior looking spare and clean but to make it feel permanent and resonant. Where detail does occur, it is found, full-bodied and at full throttle, in the form of mass, volume, and scale. Two-story columns that stop just short of the ceiling, a seventy-foot side aisle that zips the length of the house, the flight of the mezzanine across the salon—*these* are the details.

So I excavated from
an active place inside
myself—and I built it.
I love the idea of
taking your heart out
for a walk and
bringing it home.

A lilting roof of cedar shingles and an entrance
located beneath a vine-heavy pergola leading to a carriage
house gives this dwelling a gentle presence. The
honey-colored stucco, darkly mullioned windows, and
large bays recall the houses of Sir Edwin Lutyens.

I've always loved the sequence of entering a compressed, protective space before finding release into the loftiest room of the house. Even within these taller spaces, it is important to have something low enough to touch. In the salon, I designed a mezzanine so low that it almost brushed my head when I walked under it. There was a chandelier hanging in the center of the room, which I could reach from the mezzanine. When I leaned over the railing to light the candles, the salon immediately felt intimate and less voluminous. An alcove looking into the salon offers an emotional quality quite different from the rest of the room. It evokes benevolence, like the lap of someone who loves and protects you and is gesturing to the world in invitation. This is an emotion I relate to very strongly and that I like to make manifest physically. How many "I love you's" can a house hold?

My home has always been a place where I love to experiment. It is where I live my lessons. I have about a thirty-six-month cycle before I seriously start redecorating or moving altogether. In this case, I continued on in the same ship for several years, discovering how many different roles it could play. Many things were going on during those years, and I wanted the interior to be either parallel to or corrective of what I was feeling. That is what I use an interior for.

If you view these interior designs in order, the first was a self-portrait (meaning my public delivery— me at my best with everyone). What followed was the "white phase," which corresponded to a very extroverted, celebratory time—let's be brave and ridiculous—so things were a little above and beyond the conventions. There were a lot of big parties . . . and a lot of repainting. What followed, as maybe it often does, was a more introspective time. I wanted to dim the houselights and contemplate all that had just happened and what was going to be. These are the emotional tags to each stage in the design.

Previous page: A Flemish tapestry, an eighteenth-century corner chair, and a Dutch chandelier are among the carefully chosen antiques in the salon. A floor of variegated concrete pavers laid in a random ashlar pattern adds a rustic note to the refined setting. *Above:* Leaded-glass windows and lime-waxed wood cabinets lend the kitchen warmth and dignity. *Right:* Located at the entrance to the salon, the dining area becomes an integral part of the living space, rather than a room set apart and rarely used.

In the first design, there was an intention to create a lasting self-portrait. I filled the house with things I had carefully collected. It was an assembly of everything I thought to be extraordinary—things in which I saw beauty and that I believed would endure. Objects I found to be exemplary, like beautiful corner chairs, populated the rooms. I love chairs, and I really can't have enough of their different characters in a room. Standing on a stone floor, they seem somehow more important than when they are on a carpet. I liked this pairing of traditional furniture with a bare floor.

Throughout the house, there were consistently mature choices in every item, which rendered the conservative quality and timeless air I sought. But I also gave myself permission to do things that were in a way illegal, like putting a leather valence in the fireplace and spacing the mezzanine's pickets as they would have been in an old European house—shoulder-width apart and against code. Because they broke the rules, these things electrified the space.

Next, I turned the interior into a sepia-and-white photograph. I had just adopted a big, white greyhound, and I wanted the house to go with the dog, because he was a huge part of my life. Greyhounds are such beautiful poseurs. I kept a lot of the antiques, but I also added modern pieces. A very tall screen came in at this point, creating a shift of scale that made you feel just a little bit small next to it. When we are children, we love to be near the enormity of the ocean and to play in it. The screen was about evoking that kind of

Right: In the white phase of the grand salon, an eighteenth-century French barometer hangs on a twelve-foot-high screen, demonstrating McAlpine's approach to marrying rare antiques with modern design. An early twentieth-century club chair, an antique barrel-back chair, and a new sofa by the designer cluster around the stone fireplace. *Following spread, left:* White walls and upholstery accentuate the silhouettes of McAlpine's collection of antique chairs. *Following spread, right:* Cast stone floors, leaded windows, and a massive stone table add suggestions of the English country house to the sleek salon.

Folding screens enfold a daybed designed
by McAlpine where his greyhound, Joe, reclines.
Behind it, a perilously thin band of iron creates
a candle ledge spanning a wide wall of windows.

emotion. I also designed a sixteen-foot-long console of heavy stone with an almost impossibly fragile iron candle ledge above it. I told the metalsmith that I wanted it to look as if it might begin—just begin—to collapse beneath the weight of the candles. Here again is a place where the grand gesture prepares you for the vulnerable and the tender.

These elements formed a setting for what was a very expansive time. The house witnessed a lot of celebrations—the millennium, a wedding reception, gatherings of friends. It was a safe, glad place to be in and take risks. During parties, friends would slip through the mezzanine's railing and swing down to the floor below. But expansive times don't last forever. They cycle in and out. And all white schemes go. They fade out under real-life circumstances.

After the expansiveness of omitting color from the interior, I entered another period of my life. Maybe because I was feeling vulnerable, I created an architecture of exile. I wanted to pull the walls in and to wrap them around me like a blanket, creating maximum warmth. So I darkened the shell and textured it, using linseed oil mixed with pigment to give it an aged and almost stormy, turbulent presence. In my mind, this house was in some other country—an exotic place of exile—hence the map of Bohemia above the hearth. It was as if I had raided the world of its finest things and run off to the hills to hide and heal. There all the glorious contents of my treasure chest were juxtaposed against an ancient, rugged setting. It was an internalized paradise where I pulled the world down inside of me until I could figure out what I needed to do next.

In the salon's final interpretation, curtains of chocolate-brown mohair, dark velvet upholstery, and antique leather trunks create a masculine sanctuary.

Many different things were going on during those years, and I wanted those interiors to be either parallel to or corrective of what I was feeling. That is what I use an interior for.

Layers of plaster with inherent color rubbed with linseed oil lend the walls the appearance of turbulent storm clouds.

Above: Lime-waxed cypress paneling, a darkly glowing ceiling, and mohair
draperies form a richly textured backdrop for a minimalist bed designed by McAlpine.
Right: In the salon, a graphite finish gives this column a natural sheen.

COMMUNION

There is a certain honesty and simplicity about lakeside camps. They are places where things can be discovered that can't be found in town, and exchanges made that can't occur in more urban environments. This house was commissioned by a couple who wanted that kind of setting for their primary residence—a relaxed, unpretentious environment for their family and friends. In this spirit of modesty and intimacy, their house was conceived to resemble what might have been a forester's cabin in the 1920s.

To be on the water is to be a silent witness, not an intruder. That is why I wanted this house to turn a passive face toward the lake. Instead of thrusting itself toward the water, the house steps back with a low-slung shape and colors that blend into the woods. Brown planks cover the walls and gigantic green shingles shaped like leaves cover the roof. An old-fashioned reroofing shingle that people used to install when they couldn't afford a new roof, these shingles are now virtually impossible to find. I've used them several times because there is something wonderfully poetic about that Jolly Green Giant diamond shape. It's quaint and inexpensive and so very, very romantic.

Inside the house, the walls are painted almost black. Even the window mullions and sashes are that same near-black color. Unlike white sashes, which tend to stop your eye at the window, dark ones don't interrupt your engagement with nature. When you are in a deeply shaded container like this, you find yourself being drawn outward. As wonderful as it is to be on the inside, you are also constantly being lured outside by a beckoning world. You are invited into communion with nature, which is the enormous gift of this simple house.

Previous spread: With a leaf-green roof, and walls of stone, stained wood, and mullioned glass, the house provides a quiet presence on the lake beside which it stands. *This spread:* In a dynamic rhythm of opposites, waxed pine beams, hewn from trees cleared to build the house, contrast with dark walls, and a soft carpet offers luxurious counterpoint to the living room's masonry floor and stacked stone fireplace.

FRIENDSHIP

With moments of elevated stature balanced by a sweet posture, this house makes an offer of great friendship. An exaggerated piece, it spikes upward with elements of regal bearing, then immediately drifts low. After sweeping high, the roof of the house dips a bit at the top, like the swaybacked ridge of a well-aged cottage. Within a fairly humble body, French Norman windows stand erect, with tall proportions. Diffusing the grand gesture of the forward gable, an entrance at the side of the house offers a subtler invitation. At any moment, two things are occurring—one noble and the other calming and approachable. Through this rhythm of opposites, the house becomes a home and a friend.

I find it almost intimidating to enter the face of a house. To be able to slip in sideways allows even a meek soul to enter. In my great appreciation of the language of country houses, I think of the approaching face of this house as slightly disheveled and asymmetrical, and easy to find your way into. The house does not show itself as a disciplined and gorgeous thing until you reach the garden face. If the front of this house came on as strong as the rear, you might never enter in the first place.

With one eye open and one closed, it has a charming, half-awake quality. It only becomes wide-eyed and celebratory at the end of the story. The house is like a great friendship or marriage or love affair that is even more ravishing to look back upon than to walk toward. It is an easy invitation with a beautiful, important finale.

Though unpretentious, this house is not unproud. You might call it a cottage of great pride.

The asymmetry of the sideways entrance, tall chimneys topped with unmatched chimney pots, and a welcoming over-door canopy offset the imposing verticality of the house.

The side porch, with its conical roof, and a garden shed
shaped like a dovecote add charming grace notes.

REVELATION

The desire my clients and I had for this house was that it be as accessible and elegant as an Anglican country church or cottage. In turning its humblest face to the street, it reserves its magnitude until you are known to it. Because the house is intended to pull back sweetly from the outside world, the forward part is only one story high and contains just a single room. Following the line of the sloping lot, it stands twice as tall at the rear. When you discover this elevation, the house comes to fruition and reveals its petite grandeur. As in a great friendship, it holds back at the beginning in order to be approachable. But in the last act, it gives of itself with great generosity, revealing what a beautiful place you are in.

From the street, the house resembles a small, low cottage flanked by outbuildings. On the rear facade, however, a two-story window and two tall wings with wrought-iron balcony rails soar high atop the hilltop setting.

A bridge connects the house to an octagonal wing with a bell-shaped roof. Poised above a pool cabana, the living room/dining room is furnished with both glazed and screened French doors that transform it into an all-weather gazebo.

AQUEOUS

A passage tunneling beneath groin vaults, the entrance gallery to this house is a bit like the canal-level entrance to a Venetian palazzo. Part of the language of transportation and transience, groin vaults are meant to be experienced on your way to somewhere else. With a kind and compressive embrace, they are soft and heavy to the same degree. However lovely, these vaults create an environment that you want to inhabit momentarily . . . not indefinitely.

The entrance gallery prepares you for a rapturous staircase that ascends to the piano nobile. Illuminated by sky and ocean and sand, the lofty rooms on the second level offer the perfect correction to the compressed space below. As you rise from the groin-vaulted passage to this upper floor, you get the feeling that you are emerging into the air and light, almost as though you had been deep underwater. Upon entry, you are swimming, but by the time you get to the top of the stairs, you are walking.

Throughout the interior, there was a desire to invoke the illusion that the rooms are populated by objects found beneath the sea. High treasure, they are gorgeous and precious things, salvaged not as much from another era as from a parallel universe. Immensely theatrical, they mesmerize, imparting a certain otherworldly glamour.

Much of the furniture and accoutrements in this seaside villa have a sun-washed, sea-sprayed patina, including this pair of antique wood sea horses and a stone bust of Neptune.

Throughout the interior, there was a desire to invoke the illusion that the rooms are populated by objects found beneath the sea.

Venetian plaster walls and a pecky cypress ceiling create a burnished setting for gleaming details, including a gilded Venetian chair and a chandelier composed of Italian and French elements. A fragment of a ship's prow hangs above the mantel in overt reference to the sea that lies beyond the salon's windows.

Decorated in tones inspired by pears, this morning room offers cool contrast to the bright beach outside. While the bleached wooden legs of a table found at the Paris flea market recall sun-whitened driftwood, the green palette refreshes the eye.

FOLLY

When it was just a big, featureless pasture, this parcel of land was given to the city of Montgomery for a cultural park. Pretty much given carte blanche to populate it with buildings, we created follies whose primary purpose was to be evocative and poetic. First we dug a pond—so that in crossing it, you would be transported into a different reality. Spanning it, a primitive stone bridge sets the mood for the sheer timelessness and placeless-ness of the park. You could be in Norman France or Elizabethan England.

Midway across the pond an abandoned thunder house with an erratic gable of staggered stone blocks guards the bridge. I love the notion of parapets that look like the work whistle blew and the stoneworkers left and never came back to finish. Hope for the future—and the past—lies in their unchiseled blocks. They issue the imagination a subtle invitation to finish the story.

With a curious form and no function, the tower is even more of a folly than the bridge. Built onto a skid, it can actually move around the park, towed by a tractor. When it moves, people have to hunt for it—where did the tower go? Starting out at the bottom as an octagon, then becoming a square, and then a cone, the tower just wanted to flower in a certain way. I knew it had to be small and potent. Thatch, organic and sculptural, seemed to be the right roofing material for this little mushroom of a building.

Shaggy silvering thatch also covers the roof of a timber-frame theatre across the park. Unlike the tower, the theatre is rooted into the ground with heavy timbers and a low roof. Patiently anticipating actors and an audience, it reminds me of an old and bony Irish wolfhound, who waits in uncanny silence for his master to return.

Previous spread and this spread: Rough-cut Alabama stone, sandblasted and slathered with mortar, lends the appearance of ancient ruins to the park's bridge and thunder house.

Blount Cultural Park

Formal Dedication
July 22, 2002

Richard B. Cheney
Vice President of the
United States

Heavy timbers and roofs of Turkish reed laid by Irish thatchers
give the theatre and rest area soft, organic silhouettes.

There is a rhythm established by the theatre's very grand opening on one side and the humble threshold opposite, where the thatch roof is so low you can reach up and touch it. It is a gesture of reassurance on the outer edge of the theatre's deep cavern.

II

THE WAY WITHIN

I'm very drawn to the idea of a house that doesn't have a true front door. In a conventional house with a door that faces the sidewalk, you never really leave the street behind. Perhaps this is why I frequently design houses with the premise that you don't enter their faces. Instead, you come in through the side, or through a courtyard or a loggia hidden from the street. I love how this disengages you from the outside world. It's the idea of an interior address, as opposed to an exterior one. By the time you arrive at a place of rest, you have lost the street along the way.

Enticing you toward an unknown destination, this progression of twists and turns and spirals continues inside. Made compressive and shadowy by heavy walls or an exaggeratedly low ceiling, a foyer can both welcome you into a protective space and compel you forward. Terminating in a light-filled staircase that baits you to ascend, an entrance gallery can offer the promise of release—sensory, emotional, and even spiritual. Transforming you into a different—and better—creature, such labyrinths ready you for the curative heart of the house.

A tool of disorientation, the complex sequencing uncloaks your emotional garments, letting them fall away until you are unmasked. This process is meditative and serene. You are pulled toward something inevitable, which seems to move away from you even as you come toward it, but at a slower rate. This gradual unfolding makes way for your metamorphosis. By the time you arrive, you have lost one context and gained a new one—one where you can live most creatively.

DISCOVERY

There is an odd thing about this house, which draws you slowly into its center through many paths and passages. After so many twists and turns, you expect to explode into a huge great hall. Instead, you find yourself pausing in a room that is humble. It is not terribly deep, and the ceiling is not all that high. An unusual kind of space, it has four exposures, which is almost impossible to achieve. A bit like a garden pavilion, its expansiveness comes not from what is within, but from what surrounds it. It is the surprise at the end of the journey, a quiet place with the power to strip away your street identity and deliver you back to yourself.

If you were to diagram this house, you would notice dozens of axial alignments running through it. They are everywhere—however, the space is not about symmetry. It is as if you took something organic in posture and threaded it through with perfect mathematical interrelationships. Not having been classically conceived, the house does not have a symmetrical nature. It is simply responsive. No matter where you are walking, there is always something receiving you. Wherever you are, there is a spiritual clarity signaling you and beckoning to your heart.

Slathered brick in a pale sienna tone and terra-cotta barrel tiles create
an atmosphere of Mediterranean warmth, issuing an invitation to enter
through the garden wall's arched door into the courtyard within.

GLADNESS

I'm deeply fond of Cape Dutch architecture—there is such a gladness to it. So many of the Dutch South African houses look like drunken baby chicks with eyes too big for their faces. They have a certain naiveté—and that is part of their charm. In this case, the facade does not have those cartoon eyes, but it does have the disproportionate expressiveness you see in houses along the canals of Amsterdam. This house, although it is not really that large, has a similar ability to heighten your emotions. It offers grandeur in miniature. Like divinity candy, it delivers a concentrated experience, intensifying your awareness of your surroundings and their effects upon you.

Overscaled and potent within the context of this small building, the steep Flemish gables and apothecary windows energize you. The romantic, bell-shaped window protrudes over the sidewalk, inviting you to look up and down the street in active participation with the world. In contrast, the entrance to the house hides beneath its overhang. Passing beneath the window's thick timbers, you leave behind the sidewalk's shiny spectacle for the repose of a protected veranda. Calm and compressive, the veranda offers a welcome respite. Shimmering at its end in invitation, an open-rung staircase offers a call to adventure. I love the idea of a staircase ascending to light.

The Dutch colonial architecture of Cape Town, South Africa, inspired the bold palette of dark brown wood and white stucco over masonry. Purposefully exaggerated exterior details, including these heavy brackets, contrast with the modern style of the interior.

European colonial architecture has bloodlines that come from wealthier, more sophisticated mother countries. These get reinterpreted by settlers and natives, becoming a little naive, and almost always more charming.

BAROQUE

Inspired by a vision of how magnificent life can be, this house is built to the most exalted standards. Conceived with utter permanence—in steel and stone and plaster and slate and lead—it is practically imperishable. Fronting two streets, it has two primary faces, which, although grand, are more about being on the inside looking out than being admired from the outside. In order to preserve the expressive quality of these viewing faces, the entrance is located on the side, opening into a groin-vaulted entry hall. As is traditional in grand European houses, the stair hall is not located near the entrance. Instead it lies in deeper sequence, at the end of a gallery running laterally through the house and connecting its rooms.

This is like a grand "touring" house. It is a beautiful walk that invites you to tour it by way of galleries and stairs that allow you to witness its rooms without entering them. Prior to revealing any one room, the deep mass of the walls of the compressive groin-vaulted galleries and vestibules prepares you for moments of gorgeous release. The salon, a beautiful elliptical chamber four or five "acts" away from the entry, is the first place of rest you find. Slowly, through distance and device, it is unveiled. Held and released in this rhythm, you experience the salon and library and stairwells intensely.

With arched vaults and groin vaults, round spaces and elliptical ones, this is a shapely and voluptuous house. Portrayed by palette and configuration, its rooms offer a full menu of emotions. You have the grand elliptical salon and the perfectly square, cubelike library. Within the groin-vaulted sequence of the entry, you find the sculptural chambering of the stairwell. You can almost envision this space being flooded with people, as if it were opening night in a European opera house. Completely baroque, the house's intention is to wrap you up in itself.

The asymmetry of this facade offers an antidote to the grandeur of this European-style manor house. Enduring building materials, including finely quarried limestone walls, tumbled stone chimneys, leaded windows, and a slate roof, add a sense of history and permanence.

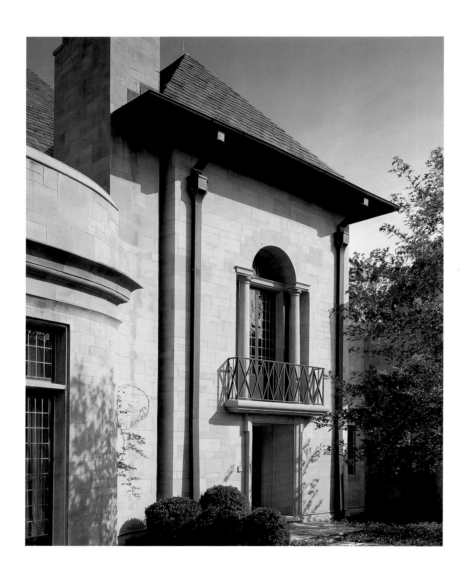

Right page: A pair of parallel side galleries lead
to the house's richly appointed rooms.

With arched vaults and groin vaults, round spaces and elliptical ones, this is a shapely and voluptuous house.

Corinthian columns, groin vaults, and Palladian door surrounds impart to the entrance hall the dignity and humanism of classical and Italian Renaissance architecture.

Perfect symmetry in both furnishings and
architectural detail create a serene atmosphere
in the elliptical salon. Pairs of carved limestone
fireplaces and gilded pier mirrors placed on
either sides of the room balance one another.

Defining three seating areas, groupings of
antique furniture calm the large space.

A dining alcove lies within a tall box bay window overlooking the grounds.
Restoration glass in leaded windows offers watery distortions of the verdant landscape
beyond and casts wavy reflections on the polished furniture and wood floor.

SKYWARD

Marking the presence of a house on a harbor, this is a landmark folly. A very serious venture into fancy, the tower has little purpose other than to elevate you—in all the meanings of that word. As you enter, a Moorish keyhole doorway at its base indicates that you are nearing the kingdom of heaven. Spiraling up the fluid sculpture of the staircase, you pass thin windows piercing the thick walls, there more to illuminate your passage than to engage you with the world outside. These are lanterns that entice you upward through the interior sequence until you suddenly burst through the wall of the tower. Delivered to the final exterior run of the staircase, you ascend to your reward—a lounge fifty feet in the air with a fireplace . . . and that magnificent view. With a chimney that yearns for the sky, the lounge is appointed by fire. It is also endowed with a bell, rung by a long rope that falls through the floor to puddle at the bottom of the stairs. A skyward pavilion built entirely of poured-in-place concrete, the tower is as poetic in reality as it was in conception. An intense endeavor for such a minimal function, it is monolithic, invincible, organic, and ethereal—all at the same time.

Constructed of poured-in-place concrete formed with a single mold,
the tower recalls both the inventive materials and unabashed romance
of early twentieth-century Mediterranean revival architecture.

Inside the tower, the nautilus spiral of concrete steps, the sinuous bronze railing, and the sway of the bell's long pull create an almost dizzying rhythm that disorients and delights.

PLACE

A lumbering slant of ground that had no intrinsic sense of place, this country property required architecture to complete it. Commissioned by clients who are enthusiastic gardeners, the house needed to ramble around, creating enclosed spaces for gardens. The house exists primarily as a device to define a sequence of outdoor rooms—gardens that are visible from anywhere within.

In the spirit of country houses, the main house is thin, light, and airy—and only one room deep. It consists primarily of two nearly identical rooms—the living room and the kitchen, either of which could contain your whole life. Split by a dogtrot-like foyer, each is a cottage and a destination unto itself. To create a sense of elegance mixed with humility, I chose wood and slathered brick for the exterior, and wood plank floors, walls, and ceilings for the interior. This is not a house of veneers, which points to the integrity of the architecture and its inhabitants.

To enter, you first pass through a covered gate into a courtyard, where the garden is presented. Then you drift sideways toward a breezeway that terminates in a door. Within this uncontained sequence of spaces, you are given several gifts before gaining entrance to the rest of the house. Deconstructed into outbuildings, garden structures, the main house, and its wings, the architecture is experiential rather than monolithic. Rapturous in its composition, it is more "place" than "object."

The low walls, shallow steps, terraces, and connected buildings of this country house define as many garden spaces as interior rooms.

This is not a house of veneers,
which points to the
integrity of the architecture
and its inhabitants.

While the waxy finish of the living room's clear cypress
walls renders a satiny sheen, the opaque glaze of the pecky
cypress ceiling resembles sun-blistered paint.

French mutton-bone chairs and a heavy iron chandelier
add rustic elegance to the dining room.

Left: Antique botanical prints, the softly modern lines of the bed, and a French segmental arch leading to the master bath marry antique and modern, rural and refined style. *Following spread:* Sophisticated luxury reigns in the powder room, with glass tiles and a cast-iron urn, and in the master bath, with shield back chairs and opulent draperies.

HOSPITALITY

The essence of this house is a certain formality, clouded by devices that diminish its magnitude. Into a dwelling that is classical at its core, I imported obstacles and layers to soften it, making it less an object than an experience. Walls and outbuildings and courtyards break the magnitude of the house into pieces, slowing the approach to its more formal facade. The entrance sequence unfolds layer by layer, admitting you gradually before you are actually invited into the house itself.

To truly enter, you must pass through a gateway into a courtyard and then a garden bower. As a Southerner would first offer you something to eat or drink before seating you for dinner, the garden is offered up as an hors d'oeuvre prior to the formal hospitality of the inner sanctum. Your first experience on the inside is a classic Southern center hall, which is something I almost never do. I can only bear its propriety here because the journey inward is so convoluted.

The main house is pristine and correct, seemingly the most cared-for part of the property, in that it has the most paint on its brick. As you stray farther and farther away from the house, the illusion of weathered decay dilutes its appearance of elegant propriety. By becoming ever more unpainted and vine-covered, the outlying walls and buildings appear to grow more and more uninhabited and released back to nature. Never anything other than natural *and* classical, modest *and* important, the house is completely faithful to the character of its owners. As proper as they are in all the things they do, they are also gently approachable. For me, this was an episode in portraiture.

Right: Wide gates open to this country estate's sweeping drive where a *pigeonnier* sets a romantic mood.
Following spread: In keeping with the tradition that what touches the earth is of the earth, tumbled stone forms a foundation for part of the house and its garden walls.

The essence of
this house is a
certain formality,
clouded by devices
that diminish its
magnitude.

III

ANCIENT MODERN

The pairing of the modern with the ancient is strangely, deeply compatible. The wonderful thing about the combination is that it is inclusive—it is an embrace of what you find to be real and broad and clear and right. Modernism, as much as classicism, can be a fierce, claustrophobic religion. Diehard modernists who build modern houses filled with modern furniture are just as limited as anybody else. But if the pendulum is able to swing far to the left and the right, then a lot of things can enter and find their comfort.

It would be a violation to infuse modernism into something comprised of flannel or cotton, like a New England clapboard structure. From the beginning, it's too tender to be tampered with at the level I want to. I have to take up a more potent critter, which can bear this different interpretation or infusion. When I'm looking for something that can withstand a modern infusion, I seek an architecture with an innate, brute strength.

Ancient buildings made of stone and masonry have the potential to become beautiful ruins. When everything that was tenuous and temporal erodes and is worn down to the bone, a spare, naked essence is revealed. I love to create the illusion of an ancient place peeled back to this point of ruin, then re-infuse it and carbonate it with modernism. I once invented the brick vestiges of a beautiful Flemish-style building that had been consumed by fire. When its baroque brick gables were transformed by sidewalls and a roof of glass, it became a Victorian conservatory. It was as if what was perishable perished, and what returned was the ghost of the original—a modern ghost made of glass and steel.

We live in an evolved architecture mostly comprised of veneers and trims—paneling, baseboards, crown moldings, window casings, you name it. It is all appliqué. When you visit a monastery or castle, it is not an architecture of veneer—it is the real thing. When stone walls hit a stone floor without appliqué or trim, there's a resounding truth. It is at once as ancient as it is modern.

PAVILION

Hidden within a traditional expression, this house has an arrestingly modern character. It is as if an Italian garden pavilion that was never meant to be enclosed was sealed and conditioned for living in the twentieth century. Envisioning this change taking place in the modern age, I used factory sash windows, which have an industrial kind of elegance. Sliding between pairs of freestanding columns, they form a transparent wall, offering insight into the house's modernism.

Strong willed and strong blooded, the ancient aspects of the Mediterranean style can take it when you hit them hard with glass walls and thin factory frames. Moments of pure fantasy balanced by modern arrangement and appointments infuse the antique elements of the pavilion's design. Rarely—if ever—expressed in unalloyed modernism, this blending of seemingly disparate languages is compelling and inclusive, advancing the traditional palette of architecture forward.

My vision was that life would take place in one very complex room—complex not by virtue of its architecture, but by the nature of its program. I imagined all dining, lounging, and cooking happening within a seventy-foot-long cruciform-shaped shell. What would have been four rooms became one, with different activities divided only by drapery and furniture. This unfettered treatment of space respects the house's pavilion nature, as does the seamless relationship between the interior and the world beyond its windows.

This room does not feel like a finite enclosure. Windows and doors open in obvious invitation. Even the walls offer just a hazy suggestion of solidity. Entirely tattooed in pencil, they seem to pulse, blurring your perception of containment. What is not glass is written word or hieroglyph. Neither wall nor window, it is text. The effect is spellbinding and delightfully disorienting.

Using a classical Italian structure and fusing it with 1930s factory minimalism proved a strangely compatible and beautiful pairing.

Previous spread and right: While the house resembles an ancient pavilion with a modern glass core, the entrance loggia retains an antique open-air configuration. Limestone columns and stucco groin vaults recall the classical past while a rubble stone niche adds a primitive, regional detail.

Left: An open-air bridge spans the space between the hilltop villa and the alfresco dining room in the thunder house. *Above:* Adding yet another time frame, architectural details reminiscent of the Italian Renaissance and Palladian era surround the courtyard entrance.

Strategically placed drapery and furniture, like this sofa enwrapped by tall screens, designed by McAlpine, delineate discrete spaces within the pavilion. Fluted partition walls create divisions between the salon, kitchen, and an intimate inglenook beyond.

Tattooed in pencil and ink, then veiled with a sheer glaze, the mural, by architectural painter David Braly, resembles a surrealistic frieze depicting architectural and botanical forms. Images of ripened vegetables and fruit cover the kitchen walls while acanthus leaves, within which the family crest is hidden, decorate the dining area's walls.

Cypress paneling conceals the shower and toilet room in the master bathroom. A cast-concrete vanity and factory sash windows provide a modern contrast to the travertine marble parquet floor.

A massive fifteenth-century bed dominates the guest bedroom. European antiques and antique-white oak floorboards of uneven width enhance the room's aura of great age, offset by the metal mullions of the factory sash windows.

ROMANCE

This is one of the very few houses I've designed that began with an exterior. During their honeymoon in France, my clients fell in love with an old gatehouse. They dreamed about living there for twelve years before asking me to design a house inspired by it. There is always something romantic when someone envisions living in a converted barn or carriage house. Scaled more for gregarious, energetic tasks than domestic ones, these places can be modest and quietly grand at the same time.

Inspired by a building designed for vehicles and animals, the house breaks pattern with the usual residential plan. It does not offer a slow, gradual invitation. Things come fast, as so often happens in rural structures. The front door opens directly into a vast, multipurpose room scaled for carriages that once would have passed through it. It is not chambered like a formal room. Instead, the gallery, living room, and dining area are all one, divided only by rustic timber posts. These are not meant to be decorative or programmatic—they are there simply to hold the structure up.

To calm the space, I created the biggest fire-mouth I could. When things become that massive, they have a quieting force. The same thing happens in the master bedroom. Large panels wrap around the bed with a kind of benevolence that holds and protects. These are the hosts that tame the animal nature of these rooms, making them habitable and hospitable.

Originating from an archetype that was never meant to be residential, the house marries the utilitarian with the domestic. This is the source of both its modernism and romance. Inviting freedom from convention, this kind of architectural recycling can be stimulating. It cracks everything open and feeds a lot of creativity, allowing for an inclusive interior where things of many different natures coexist.

The oak grate above the door leading from the living room to the stairs helps tell the story that the stair hall was once an open-air passage connecting the carriage house to the adjacent porte cochere.

Massive brackets and timbers support the ceiling, another reminder of the structure's fictional agricultural past. Curvaceous furniture, including a fluted concrete console, an antique sofa with undulating legs and braces, and waist stools, echo the line of the brackets, softening the room's intentional austerity.

Originating from an archetype that was never meant to be residential, the house marries the utilitarian with the domestic. This is the source of both its modernism and romance.

Kitchen doors open to a space intended to resemble a primitive porte cochere. Its rustic stone wall serves as the backdrop for a curtain of water that creates a soothing ambiance in this indoor/outdoor sitting room. Industrial chairs that surround a replica of the kitchen table in Sir Edwin Lutyen's Castle Drago demonstrate an eccentric mix of objects that lends a modern air.

Expressed with extreme simplicity of line, the
barrel vault and bay window create a surprisingly
modern appearance in the master bedroom.

Above: Large cabinets with glazed cypress doors provide ample storage in a mixed-purpose room used for laundry, arranging flowers, and projects. *Right:* A copper faucet automatically flows into the powder room's antique marble sink when someone enters the room.

INVITATION

What you see in this house is a close fusion of modern thought and familiar form. If given a natural way to tilt, I'm going to lean toward architecture that is English or Scottish. With a kind and malleable will, these styles offer an anti-classicist solution that is based in romance. Because the language of these houses seems sometimes too tender to modernize, I relished the opportunity to travel in this new ground.

The first rooms you encounter issue an invitation, asking you to complete them. Modern in their scale and proportions, the foyer and grand salon are cavernous and almost empty. They are the better for your presence. Somewhere in the clients' vision was a desire not to choke these spaces but to leave them in a state of readiness for entertainments and celebrations.

The tendency in a large, voluminous room is to float groupings of furniture in the center. In the regal, billowing space of the salon, intimacy is found in the corners and against the walls in high-backed upholstered alcoves. The minute you do something overstated and exhilarating, an apology of sorts must come right on its heels. The humble has to be in the presence of its opposite. It's an odd little emotion that seeks asylum in the midst of grandeur. Where can I exist in this gorgeous space? The answer is within an alcove.

Very often I put the dining room in a passage. There it loses all potential to become stilted. Placed in the heart of the house, it becomes a touchstone for the life that goes on around it. It becomes a vessel for memory—and memory has to do with pattern. The mapping of trips and eating of food and convening with friends and family take place around the table. When you graze it as you pass by, which you must constantly do, you touch the place where most things have been said and ideas formed and voyages planned. I like that much more than the dining table being just a destination. It opens the door for broader exchange.

Three vertical windows, each concealing a large door, bring bright light into the grand salon and open to allow guests to enjoy the terrace beyond. Throughout the house, similar metal-and-glass windows and doors add modern undertones to the house's stucco-over-masonry walls, slate roof, and copper downspouts.

Large expanses of glass, the rhythmic intersection of walls and eaves, and a long pool with a charcoal-colored concrete interior create a strong impression of modernism at the rear of the house.

The minute you do
something overstated
and exhilarating,
an apology must come
right on its heels.
The humble has to
be in the presence
of its opposite.

A sequence of barrel vaults ripples across
the ceiling of the grand salon, accentuating the
room's height while softening its contours.

Above: Artwork from the residents' collection, antique chairs, and contemporary banquettes designed by McAlpine furnish intimate corners of the salon. *Right:* A combination of glazed and screened doors turns the informal lounge area into an all-season pavilion.

Above: Fluted cabinets offer a contemporary impression of antique linen-fold paneling in the kitchen.
Right: A light-filled gallery passes by the kitchen to terminate in the dining room. The mezzanine above invites natural illumination and air into the residents' home offices.

In the dining room, reeded cabinetry holds
books, artwork, and family photographs, establishing
an atmosphere of warmth and lives well lived.

Sitting beneath a massive oak chimney breast and flanked by factory sash windows, an inviting inglenook offers a place of intimacy and repose within the expansive family living room.

INVISIBLE

This commission for an addition to a Georgian revival house began with a request for a dining room that seated one hundred guests. How do you stick something that large onto an existing house? The answer was to create something invisible—or rather, something that seems to have disappeared.

I started the design with two brick Flemish gables. It looked as if a fire had destroyed the original structure long ago, leaving only the gables behind. Following the baroque shape of the gables, glass walls and a glass ceiling enclose the huge space. Transforming the Flemish ruins into a conservatory, they might have been added in the Victorian age. Hanging between the gables, they are like ghosts of antique walls. But they are also crisp, lighthearted, and modern.

There is a way of folding modernism into something with a more mature execution that makes everything the better for it. It wakes up those things that look ancient without sacrificing their essence. The brick walls, which appear to be so old, seem all the more wise and imperishable next to the fragile glass. The sheer curtain walls of glass seem like such a gift next to the heavy brick.

At night, prisms from the crystal chandeliers make stars on the stone floor. Silvered columns gleam in the candlelight. The brick walls melt into the shadows and the glass disappears. The solid and the invisible, and the antique and the modern, coexist in a balance that cannot be explained. It simply makes your heart pause, and even ache a little.

There is a way of folding modernism into something with a more mature execution that makes everything the better for it. It wakes up those things that look ancient without sacrificing their essence.

Silver-leafed columns and a pair of crystal chandeliers reflected in the gilded mirror above the mantel shimmer beneath both sunlight and moonlight in this conservatory-like salon. Accommodating dances, dinners, and cocktail parties, furnishings that move easily around the room include gondola chairs and custom banquettes.

GLAMOUR

There is definitely theatre and drama and rapture being tended to here. Consequently, the house and its interior come off a bit like the set of an early motion-picture show or a glamorous 1930s movie house. Through filmmaking and set design, Hollywood created an architecture that never really existed. By borrowing freely and fusing differing ideas, its designers invented what would be most deeply affective without too much regard for what was correct. They combined and exaggerated things in order to heighten the power of the moment.

My fantasy for this house was that it resemble a palace built at the turn of the twentieth century by a railroad tycoon with fabulous wealth. As much as it is endowed with moments of tradition and elegance, it also has modern gestures that tip their hats toward the innovative spirit of the time. The three-story-high free-falling drapery in the stairwell, the tall volume of the salon and its continuous ribbon of clerestory windows—these are not the makings of a conservative, traditional residence. The weighty resonance of the salon is carbonated at the last moment by the band of windows and the baroque protrusion of the balconies—places of witness that recall the theatrical moments of great movie houses.

Sensual, playful, and dramatic, this is a place that a gregarious animal might have created as a grand setting for living. It is an enormous playhouse meant for expansive expressions of fun and celebration. Being in the house—with its many axes, alignments, titillations, and invitations—is almost like dancing a waltz. When you are not being embraced or invited to turn, you are being tapped on the shoulder. Great theatrical moments are regularly created, conjuring a setting as fantastical and glamorous as any picture show.

Previous spread: Groupings of antique European furniture create an intimate scale within the majestic proportions of the great hall. Glass doors and clerestory windows flood the room with light by day. At night, the glow from the iron chandelier creates a warm ambience. *Left:* Serpentine balconies with wrought-iron railings echo the baronial proportions of the great hall's limestone fire surround, iron lanterns, and tapestry hanging. *Above:* Beneath the shadow of a cypress ceiling, the morning room provides intimate contrast to the great hall.

In both the kitchen and dining room, ceilings of pecky cypress contribute texture, contrasting with the more polished surfaces of the surrounding floors and walls.

Above: White upholstery and a wooden ceiling finished with a pale glaze reflect the natural light to create a serene environment in the bedroom. *Right:* Limestone parquet floors, cascading curtains, a porcelain bath, and an antique *duchesse brisée* chair conjure an atmosphere of romance and luxury in the master bath.

IV

SANCTUARY FOR THE SELF

Some of the best lessons about unleashing and nurturing your truest—and perhaps most concealed—identity come in the form of second homes. Primary houses are all too often inscribed with dreams and expectations borrowed from parents or society. They tend to be houses on a street of houses, surrendering some essential aspect of their inhabitants' soul for the greater good of their surroundings. They often devote a lot of space and energy to pleasing everyone but those who dwell there.

In second homes, however, all eyes are off. So we tend to be more honest about who we are and how we would live if no one were watching. What we create in this unobserved posture is not only truer to who we are, but can also lead us into even deeper waters of discovery. By living in such a place, we ultimately develop a stronger heart muscle.

When you are fortunate enough to have more than one residence, then you have a chance to create the flip side of your primary home—maybe even the wild side. Perhaps because most second homes are built in the presence of something immense—the mountains, the ocean—the air is cleared of expectations. The way you play, and even the way you sit still, changes. This is a point of departure from which to take risks and explore, creating places that are sexier, more romantic, or more profound than our primary homes.

Even if your home is your only house, the potential still exists to break free. Be inspired by a beachside villa with a sequence of spaces that unfolds like the dance of the seven veils, ending in a haremlike porch. Dream of a bedchamber barely wide enough for one big bed, but as tall as a telephone pole. Imagine an entire house with only two interior doors, in which a husband and wife remain always within each other's sight. Seek solace in a meditation space with a gentle posture and a silence as pure as an ancient chapel in a remote English village. The invisible essence of these retreats is the idea of sanctuary—a place so sheltered, so safe, so true that you slide into easy companionship with your deepest self.

TITILLATION

To be titillated and exhilarated—that is what you look for when you are on vacation. An unlikely marriage of provincial colonial architecture with a sexy, sophisticated style, this seaside retreat offers a delicious sort of pairing. The question is how do you put these things together? I imagined a tropical paradise where a decadent Italian princess with trunks full of worldly things might have landed.

Like the dance of the seven veils, the house tantalizes you by revealing itself slowly. Above the facade's impenetrable stucco wall, a second-story porch teases you. There is no obvious way to reach it. With no front door, the facade offers only a jib door, which opens to a narrow passage along the house's side. By the time you find your way into the courtyard beyond, you feel as if you've been blindfolded and spun around. After taking another turn or two to enter the house, you are completely disoriented. It is such a queer experience that you surrender completely to its unfamiliarity. You are stunned and even feel a little drunk.

Breaking American cultural expectations, the primary rooms are located in European style on the piano nobile. In contrast to the labyrinth leading to them, they flow freely from one to the next, moving toward the balcony. Instead of rushing toward its beckoning light, however, you are invited to take your time. A sequencing of spaces asks you to linger beneath the exaggeratedly low ceiling of the living room. The sensitive animal in me always wants to sit under something low. I come to rest better that way.

Beyond the protective embrace of the living room, the world gets suddenly bigger. With a wall of glass delivering it to the world beyond the balcony, the dining room seems a vast, towering space. It is a big gesture, not solely in terms of volume. Coming unexpectedly at the end of a complex sequence, it triggers your sensual being like the end of a striptease. With complete abandon, it delivers you into the moment.

Nestled between two other houses designed by McAlpine, this seaside villa offers the cool retreat of a front porch raised well above the level of the street. Tucked beneath a galvanized aluminum roof, its louvered shutters offer privacy, shade, ocean views, and seaborne breezes to those within.

With exposed rafters painted dark, the underside of the guest room suite forms a protective ceiling in the living room. Beneath it, richly textured opulent furnishings, including a white fur rug, express a surprising degree of sophistication for a seaside getaway.

You can put the dining area in a more vulnerable setting than any other room, because when people gather around a table, their circle creates its own enclosure. They could sit down to eat in a busy intersection and make their own space.

Above: The passage paralleling the kitchen's glazed cypress island and candle tray, both designed by McAlpine, leads to the master bedroom suite. *Right:* The master bedroom can only be reached by passing through a boudoir-like chamber where a daybed stretches languorously beneath a sunny window.

PAIRING

A house can be many things, including a portrait. Inspired by one of the most beautiful and enduring pairings I have encountered, this house is a portrait of a marriage. So I envisioned it with a double gable, as a symbol of paired unity and the joining of two strong individuals. Because this was to be a place where they could enjoy the comfort of each other's company, I immediately conceived of the house in the Shingle style. Such a Saturday aesthetic—it is like a big, worn nubby sweater you wear only around the house.

Familiar and comfortable, the Shingle style always corrects moments of grandeur with elements of sweetness and humility. The gesture of steep double gables towering into the sky makes a strong and noble first impression. In contrast, the porch's huge, curvaceous brackets are overstated, almost to the level of comedy—and that is the point. The most naive and incorrect features in Shingle-style houses are often the most charming and engaging.

A big New York-style loft interior with a soaring ceiling and a completely open floor plan—that is the surprise inside the house. With only two doors, the interior is saturated with light that flows, uninterrupted. Visible from and vulnerable to the downstairs, the upper rooms invite words and glances to travel through open spaces. Because they adore being in sight of each other, the clients love this communicative aspect. This is a place the couple longed for. On moonlit nights, they often stand outside to watch the shadow of the twin gables on the lawn.

An old-fashioned breezeway links the main house with the combined carriage house/guest suite. While gray shingles and white trim reflect the serene side of the Shingle style, the rhythmic pattern of windows and overhanging eaves expresses its exuberance.

I rarely work in a single style. With intuition as my guide, I borrow freely from the entire language of architecture.

HARBORAGE

Filled with calm composure and cool modernism, this coastal retreat resounds with unexpected moments of dissonance, resolution, and sheer romanticism. Witness the exaggerated narrowness and height of the entrance door, which prepares the visitor for the resolve waiting on the other side. You must literally pass through the eye of the needle in order to enter into heaven. Within, the house immediately welcomes you with a room offering rest and repose. Here, you are healed.

As tall as this room is, the space also unfolds horizontally, pulling you deep into its peaceful harbor. A long curtain of glass running past the shadowy room accompanies this journey. An odd symphony of things seems to be going on here. The house exudes an attitude that is both romantic *and* classically modern. The glass wall roars seamlessly past the open salon into the ground-floor sleeping area. No traditional privacy door exists for this chamber. An open mezzanine lined with sleeping berths hangs above the room. These are all modern devices.

In the presence of this, intimately scaled elements express the other end of the spectrum. Kitchen and fireside areas exist quietly under intimate seven-foot-high ceilings, in deep contrast to the cavernous space they parallel. Instead of the expected modernist plate glass, colonial-style panes divide the glass curtain wall. These devices break down the scale dramatically. They calm the thunder.

The goal of the classic modern house is to thrust you into a relationship with the environment outside of it. I always have an equal desire to befriend the inside. This haven is a pairing of the brave with the tender.

When you pass through the narrowness of the front door, you enter a room that is all about rest and repose and cure and healing. The house is its own kind of sanctuary.

Southern vernacular elements, including a galvanized aluminum roof and a long side porch, are interwoven with unexpected details, like telephone poles posing as columns, to express a postmodern approach to combining historical styles.

This haven is a
pairing of the brave
with the tender.

A pendant light illuminates an intimate lounge
tucked beneath the shelter of a loftlike guest mezzanine.
These interiors were designed by Betsy Brown.

The matte finish of a concrete dining table, also designed by McAlpine,
contrasts with the reflective sheen of the polished concrete floor.

Sheer draperies falling from the seventeen-foot-high ceiling and huge windows and door
that fill an entire wall accentuate the dramatic verticality of the master bedroom.

NAIVETÉ

A little bohemian house handmade from scraps, this cabin acquired its name—The Shack—as soon as I saw it. Clinging to the side of a steep hill in the woods, it has the soul of a riverbank cabin. I was immediately attracted to its complete lack of pretension and its internalized charm. By giving it dignified windows and doors and appointments, I renovated it to its highest form without tampering with its soul.

In those days, I was seeking a kind of somber containment in a house. I loved being in a dark shell—its compression and enclosure. The cabin had such a cratelike nature that it was impossible to resist putting gilt and fine things in its presence. It was a beautiful foil for things unlike itself. And so there was a lesson somewhere for me in the pendulum's swing between rough plank walls and gilt frames, great tapestries and absolutely raw floors.

There was an infectious friendliness about the place that was not missed by anyone who came upon it. It was intrinsically and forever humble, hence its name, The Shack. The extreme modesty of the name was mostly true, but partly in fun, because it really was a grand little place.

Previous page: Fine French tapestry cartoons hang from the walls of this rustic hillside retreat, juxtaposing European refinement against the primitive country setting. *This spread:* A screened porch supported by dark-stained telephone poles hangs above the carport. At once rough-hewn and sophisticated, stairs made from pine blocks lead to a trapdoor in the porch's floor.

Tapestry curtains and an unusually long antique French sofa are among the many rare and refined
pieces cozying up to stacked firewood and a Tennessee-stone fireplace in the living room.

Above: Four photographic prints of dogs hang above an antique French table in the master bedroom. *Right:* Curtained on all sides and just large enough for two lounge chairs, this room offers a safe den in which to rest and relax.

There was a lesson somewhere there for me in the pendulum's swing between rough plank walls and gilt frames, great tapestries and absolutely raw floors.

In the master bathroom, broken slabs of marble form the shower's walls, balancing the room's simple pine floor and walls with a note of luxury and decadence.

HUMILITY

I'm so drawn to rural English architecture, and particularly to the little churches. There is a dear trait I recognize in them that is quite absent among other church types. Most English country churches are entered from the side and not from the street. It is a very human, kind gesture that allows you to enter unnoticed. It is the opposite of the classical approach—the big, bold church with its front projecting to the street. This is the picturesque ideal. You can enter the scene without participating in a spectacle. To me, that is so sweet and invitational.

This is a quality I tapped in this building. As much as the roof soars up from the rolling eaves—an effect that is exaggerated by the chapel's miniature scale—it also does the opposite. It goes down to the grass. It lowers its head to be petted. It does everything in its power to make you feel safe in walking toward it. It is all about posture.

You enter into the chapel by way of a side aisle—a shadowy tunnel that parallels the vaulted sanctuary. You can peer into the greater space, but the ceiling hovers just above your head, creating a sense of protection. Being in the lap of something that makes you feel secure—while you are also in communication with something expansive and invitational—allows you to experience humility and grandeur at the same time.

This same rhythm occurs in the sanctuary itself, where casement windows open directly at ground level. You are actually *in* the ground, yet drawn upward by the vaulted ceiling. Immersed in a pairing of inertia and ascension, you surrender to the spirit of the chapel and reencounter your soul.

Like an old country church in the Cotswolds, this chapel was constructed by craftspeople working with age-old materials, including slate and local stone, in traditional methods. Even the lock was newly forged by a locksmith working in the time-honored manner of his trade.

Inside the chapel, Irish Chippendale-style chairs, a gilded lectern, and an altar made from an antique chest marry humble and exalted materials and forms.

A copy in miniature of a stained-glass panel given by the chapel's owners to the Folger Shakespeare Library in Washington, D.C., the brilliantly colored window set in the side aisle door honors an ancestor who published the first Shakespeare folio in 1625.

I wanted this space
to feel absolutely
permanent—as if it
had been a part
of this earth forever.

ACKNOWLEDGMENTS

This book would not exist without the generosity, kindness, vision, talent, and contributions of many people; most importantly the homeowners who helped dream these houses into being. You traveled the road to find me and commissioned a heart's dream. I am better for it. You have accompanied and enriched my own journey homeward, inviting me to live more deeply and passionately in the world.

Boundless love and gratitude go to my staff at McAlpine Tankersley Architecture, who helped transform these dreams into realized dimensions. To my partners: Greg Tankersley, John Sease, and Chris Tippett. And dedicated staff: Richard Norris, David Baker, Scott Torode, Jennifer Druhan, Charlie Caldwell, Lida Sease, and Jonathan Torode—you are not just co-workers to me, but my family and friends.

McAlpine, Booth & Ferrier Interiors dressed these dreams with ravishing imagination. Thank you to my partners Ray Booth and Susan Ferrier along with Brynna Spain, Peter Fleming, Mary Girton, Shelley Takas, Jessica Moore, Lindsay Wilkerson, Rachel Wells, Liz Bonesio, and Betty Moore.

To those who worked together on the writing, design, and publication of this book, I offer many thank-yous. Deep gratitude goes to Richard Norris, who has given body and soul to this project; to my brilliant co-writer Susan Sully, who painted my musings with her bottomless well of talent and understanding; graphic designer Doug Turshen, the epicentral genius of this project, and his staff, particularly Steve Turner; and to Hilary Ney, who helped spark the genesis of this book. Thanks to principal photographer and friend Mick Hales and contributing photographers Tria Giovan, Eric Piasecki, Peter Vitale, William Waldron, Antoine Bootz, Don Freeman, and Mark L. Wright. Your talent and artistry are the light of this book. A special thank-you to Tria, who said the right thing at the right moment that led to this book, and Kris Kendrick for her assistance with our photography library.

A special acknowledgment is given to all the editors and magazines that have painted us forward through publication: especially Lisa Newsom, founder and editor-in-chief, *Veranda*; Stephen Drucker, editor-in-chief, *House Beautiful*; and Karen Carroll, editor-in-chief, *Southern Accents*. You have invested in us tirelessly and consistently since our earliest days in business. We would never have been invited to do so many commissions without you. You are our patrons as well. Thank you, too, for allowing us to reprint images from your publications within these pages.

And finally, thank you to Rizzoli International Publications Senior Editor Sandy Gilbert Freidus, our beacon of light in the publishing world, who embraced us and this project from the beginning and graced it with her talent, expertise, and perfection; and to Publisher Charles Miers who saw and believed in the soul of this work.

To all I say, bring it on. Together we may find our way home, again.

PHOTOGRAPHY CREDITS

Antoine Bootz: pages 21, 22, 23 (courtesy of *Southern Accents*)

Don Freeman: pages 107, 108–109, 110–111, 112, 113, 114–115, 116, 117 (courtesy of *House Beautiful*)

Tria Giovan: pages 2 (courtesy of *Veranda*), 37 (courtesy of *Southern Accents*), 81, 82–83, 84–85, 208–209, 210–211, 212–213, 214, 215, 216, 217 (courtesy of *House Beautiful*)

Mick Hales: endpapers and pages 5, 6, 8, 13, 17, 18–19, 25, 26, 27, 31, 32–33, 34, 35, 38–39, 40, 41, 43, 44–45, 46, 47, 49, 50, 51, 52, 53, 64–65, 66, 67, 68, 69, 70–71, 75, 76, 77, 78–79, 87, 88, 89, 90, 91, 92–93, 94–95, 96–97, 98, 99, 101, 102, 103, 104–105, 119, 120–121, 122–123, 124–125, 129, 130–131, 132–133, 135, 136, 137, 138, 139, 140–141, 142, 143, 145, 146, 147, 148, 149, 150–151, 152–153, 154, 155, 157, 158, 159, 160, 161, 162–163, 164, 165, 166, 167, 168–169, 170–171, 173, 174–175, 176–177, 191, 192–193, 201, 202–203, 204–205, 207, 218, 220, 221, 222, 223, 224, 225, 226–227, 229, 231, 232, 233, 234, 235, 236–237

Richard Norris: page 230

Eric Piasecki: pages 55, 56, 57, 58–59, 60, 61 (courtesy of *House Beautiful*)

Karim Shashi-Basha: page 63 (courtesy of *Southern Accents*)

Peter Vitale: pages 134, 179, 180, 181, 182, 183, 184, 185, 186, 187 (courtesy of *Veranda*)

William Waldron: pages 194, 195, 196–197, 198, 199 (courtesy of *Southern Accents*)

Mark L. Wright: pages 28–29

First published in the United States of America in 2010
by Rizzoli International Publications, Inc.
300 Park Avenue South
New York, New York 10010
www.rizzoliusa.com

2010 2011 2012 2013 / 10 9 8 7 6 5 4 3 2

Printed in Singapore
ISBN 13: 978-0-8478-3289-7

Library of Congress Control Number: 2009940393

Project Editor: Sandra Gilbert
Art Direction: Doug Turshen with Steve Turner

Endpapers: Flemish gables and softly faded paint lend an air of mystery
and romance to the garden dependency of a country estate.